★ *GREAT SPORTS TEAMS* ★

THE SEATTLE

SUPERSONICS

BASKETBALL TEAM

David Aretha

Enslow Publishers, Inc.

44 Fadem Road   PO Box 38
Box 699   Aldershot
Springfield, NJ 07081 Hants GU12 6BP
USA   UK

http://www.enslow.com

Library of Congress Cataloging-in-Publication Data

Aretha, David.
    The Seattle SuperSonics basketball team / David Aretha.
        p. cm. — (Great sports teams)
    Includes bibliographical references (p. 43) and index.
    Summary: Surveys the history of the Seattle SuperSonics professional
basketball team, covering key players and coaches as well as some of the
team's great games.
    ISBN 0-7660-1102-X
    1. Seattle SuperSonics (Basketball team)—History—Juvenile literature.
[1. Seattle SuperSonics (Basketball team)—History. 2. Basketball—History.]
I. Title. II. Series.
GV885.52.S4A74   1999
796.323'64'09797772—dc21   98-19228
                                            CIP
                                            AC

To Our Readers:
All Internet addresses in this book were active and appropriate when we
went to press. Any comments or suggestions can be sent by e-mail to
Comments@enslow.com or to the address on the back cover.

Illustration Credits: AP / Wide World Photos.

Cover Illustration: AP / Wide World Photos.

CONTENTS

*D*riving for the lay-up, Sonics guard Dennis Johnson moves past Wes Unseld of the Washington Bullets.

THE COMEBACK

All through the summer of 1978, Seattle SuperSonics point guard Dennis Johnson (known to fans as D. J.) relived his nightmare game of June 7. Oh, what a horrible game it was: the worst of his career, coming at the worst of times.

Do Or Die

We are talking about Game 7 of the 1978 NBA Finals—Seattle vs. Washington. The series had been a rugged war. The young, scrappy Sonics banged chests with the bruising Bullets, a football team in sneakers.

Johnson, one victory away from fulfilling his ultimate dream, was pumped for Game 7—perhaps too pumped. On his first shot of the game, the ball banged off the rim. He missed his next shot, too, and the next and the next. His teammates kept Seattle in the game, but Johnson's bricks were sinking the ship. When the final buzzer sounded, D. J. had launched 14 shots and missed them all. Washington won, 105–99.

The experience would have crushed a lesser man, but Johnson was used to tough times. One of sixteen children, Johnson grew up poor in Los Angeles. Kids teased him because he had a freckled face and reddish hair. He was never a big star in high school or at Pepperdine University, and he barely made the Seattle roster as a rookie in 1976.

Learning From Defeat

Four months after the nightmare game, Johnson entered the 1978–79 season more determined than ever. He raised his game to a new level. His scoring average shot up from 12.7 to 15.9 points per game. He hounded opponents so intensely that he was voted to the NBA's All-Defensive first team. He even played in the All-Star Game.

Throughout 1978–79, Sonics coach Lenny Wilkens had his men playing inspired team basketball. Guards Gus Williams and "Downtown" Freddie Brown swished rainbow jumpers. Center Jack Sikma and forward Paul Silas ruled the boards. And forwards Lonnie Shelton and John Johnson scored in double figures. Together, they had the best record in the West (52–30) and were the best defensive team in the NBA.

"We weren't respected last season," Johnson said before the 1979 playoffs. "But our adrenaline flowed into momentum, a piece stuck in everybody, and it's all still with us."[1]

*S*eattle's Jack Sikma tries to tap the ball away from Bullets center Elvin Hayes.

Playoff Drive

The Sonics defeated the Los Angeles Lakers in their first series of the 1979 playoffs, four games to one. Seattle then gutted out a seven-game victory over

Phoenix by winning the last two games. They returned to the NBA Finals. Their opponent: Washington.

Johnson had the perfect chance to redeem himself, but then fate struck again. In Game 1, with the score 97–97, Washington's Larry Wright attempted a jumper with one second left. He missed, but referee Earl Strom blew a whistle. D. J., he indicated, had slapped Wright's wrist. With no time on the clock, Wright went to the line and sank two free throws. Washington won, and Johnson was the goat again.

Seattle players complained about the questionable foul call. "We were robbed," groaned John Johnson.[2] But D. J. remained tight-lipped. "It costs money [a fine] to complain about the refs," he said.[3]

Taking Over

Instead of sulking, Johnson dug down deep. From that point on, wrote Roland Lazenby, "it was about to become Dennis Johnson's series."[4] Seattle won Game 2, 92–82, as Johnson and Williams put the defensive whammy on Washington's guards. In Game 3, Johnson contributed 17 points, 9 rebounds, and disruptive defense. Williams drained 31, Sikma ripped down 17 boards, and Seattle won, 95–85.

In Game 4, an overtime thriller, this trio starred again. Williams tallied 36 points, while Sikma yanked down another 17 rebounds. Johnson scored 32 points, including 4 in overtime. The game ended when he blocked a Kevin Grevey shot before the buzzer. "I think the knockout punch was delivered tonight," Brown said.[5]

oach Lenny Wilkens and guard "Downtown" Freddie Brown hold up the NBA championship trophy. It was the first professional sports title for the city of Seattle.

How Sweet It Is

One victory away from the NBA title, Johnson seized the moment in Game 5. He continued his relentless defense and scored 13 second-half points, including two "remarkable acrobatic baskets" late in the game.[6] Seattle won, 97–93, and became the new NBA champion. Champagne flowed in the locker room, while D. J. and Williams lit up victory cigars. Johnson was named NBA Finals Most Valuable Player.

One year after his nightmarish performance, Johnson had found full redemption. "We weren't going to lose," he said. "Not this time. No way."[7]

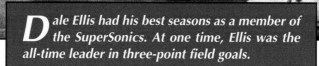

*D*ale Ellis had his best seasons as a member of the SuperSonics. At one time, Ellis was the all-time leader in three-point field goals.

COLORFUL CHARACTERS

There has always been something super-sonically cool about Seattle's professional basketball team. Why? Perhaps it's the team's hip location: Seattle, Washington, that drizzly town tucked in America's upper-left-hand corner. It's the home of grunge rock, fresh lobster, and all the coffee you can sip.

An Exciting Blend

In their thirty-plus years in Seattle, the Sonics have enjoyed considerable success: a winning overall record, three trips to the NBA Finals, and one NBA championship (1979). Moreover, few teams have ever boasted a more exciting assortment of players.

Start with some of history's great gunners. Dale Ellis had, at one time, drained more three-pointers than anyone else in NBA history. Ricky Pierce and Eddie Johnson riddled opponents with deadly, automatic jump shots. And you can't forget about "Downtown" Freddie Brown, whose nickname says it all.

You want cool? Spencer Haywood wowed Washingtonians with his sweet-butter jumper and his swift slashes to the goal. Slick "Prince of Pilfer" Watts always wore a bright-green headband on his shaved head. David "Skywalker" Thompson owned a superhuman vertical leap of forty-four inches. And then there's Shawn Kemp, who smoked the highlight reel with powerful, electrifying slam dunks.

A Rough Start

When Seattle first joined the NBA for the 1967–68 season, however, most of the highlights were on the other side of the court. In the SuperSonics' very first game, on October 13, 1967, the San Francisco Warriors rang up 144 points. Two months later, Philadelphia scored 160!

Still, the early Sonics boasted stars of their own: Bob Rule, a Mack truck in shorts, averaged 22.2 points and 10.4 rebounds from the 1967–68 to 1969–70 seasons. In 1969, Seattle hired legendary point guard Lenny Wilkens to be the team's player/coach. "Wilkens had mental toughness," said NBA coach Dick Motta.[1] Wilkens captured MVP honors at the 1971 All-Star Game. In 1971–72, he led Seattle to its first winning season, finishing 47–35.

The Sonics, it seemed, could not win without Wilkens. They traded him to Cleveland in August 1972, then wallowed in mediocrity for five years. When they started 5–17 in 1977–78, they rehired Coach

The Seattle SuperSonics Basketball Team

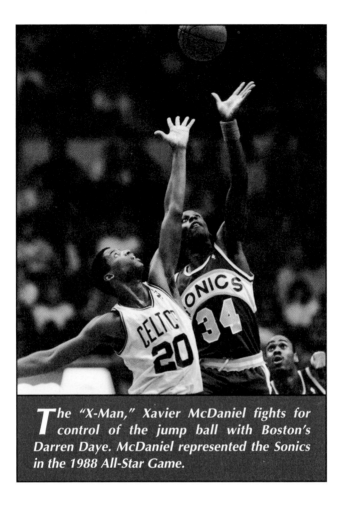

The "X-Man," Xavier McDaniel fights for control of the jump ball with Boston's Darren Daye. McDaniel represented the Sonics in the 1988 All-Star Game.

Wilkens to bail them out. Wilkens's team went 42–18 the rest of the way and stormed to the NBA Finals.

Winning Time

That Sonics' team featured the outstanding guard trio of Freddie Brown, Dennis Johnson, and Gus Williams. Jack Sikma and Marvin Webster did the damage inside. The Sonics lost to Washington in seven games, but they earned a rematch in 1978–79.

Colorful Characters

"The difference from last year is maturity," said Wilkens. "Last year we were so young, we played on emotion. There were questions. Now we run strictly on confidence."[2] Johnson and Williams played ferociously on both sides of the court in the 1979 NBA Finals. The Sonics bit the Bullets in five games for the NBA title.

High-Octane Fuel

The 1980s featured some offensive fireworks but not much success. Ellis, Tom Chambers, and Xavier McDaniel lit it up often but packed it up early. By the end of the decade, it seemed the Sonics were on a road to Nowheresville. Coach Bernie Bickerstaff went 41–41 in 1989–90. K. C. Jones finished 41–41 in 1990–91, then started 1991–92 at 18–18. Interim coach Bob Kloppenburg went 2–2.

Finally, on January 23, 1992, the Sonics hired their savior. George Karl, an eccentric, turbulent coach, revved up Seattle and went 27–15 the rest of the way. Karl relied on All-Stars Kemp and Gary Payton, a half-dozen role players, and a pressure-cooker defense. "Karl had a team ready to blast off for some serious space-aged flying," wrote Peter Bjarkman.[3]

Championship Contenders

From 1992–97, Karl's Sonics soared to new heights. Seattle went 63–19 in 1993–94, finished 64–18 in 1995–96, and charged to the NBA Finals in 1996. But the Chicago Bulls blocked their path to the NBA title.

The Seattle SuperSonics Basketball Team

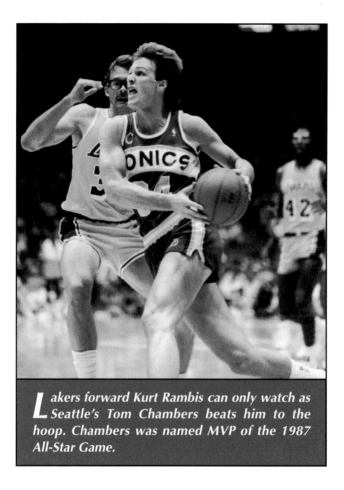

*L*akers forward Kurt Rambis can only watch as Seattle's Tom Chambers beats him to the hoop. Chambers was named MVP of the 1987 All-Star Game.

Despite just one NBA title, Sonics history is filled with excitement. One magic moment came at the 1987 All-Star Game, in front of 34,275 fans at Seattle's King-dome. The Sonics' Chambers made the West team only as a replacement for the injured Ralph Sampson. The sweet-shooting forward tallied 30 points in regulation, then added four in overtime. The West won, 154–149, in the highest-scoring All-Star Game ever. Chambers, the hometown hero, was named the game's Most Valuable Player.

Colorful Characters

*S*pencer Haywood of the Sonics tries to make room for a shot. Haywood made the All-NBA first team in 1972 and 1973.

SUPER SONICS

oincidentally, Seattle's five greatest players of all-time form a neat starting lineup. Profiled here are a multitalented point guard; a brilliant bombardier; two high-scoring, board-sweeping forwards; and a rock-steady center.

Spencer Haywood

Spencer Haywood was high style all the way. After turning pro in 1969—at age twenty—he donned a full-length fur coat and drove a Cadillac with a Rolls-Royce front. On the court, he shone like a diamond. "He was an incredible physical specimen," said opponent Mack Calvin. "He scored at ease, and he got a lot of rebounds."[1]

Haywood played his first pro season in the American Basketball Association (ABA), winning league MVP honors with Denver. He signed as a free agent with Seattle in 1970, becoming the first undergraduate player ever to enter the NBA.

From 1970–71 through 1974–75, Haywood simply dazzled Seattle. Wrote Martin Taragano: "He was a flashy, long-legged, long-armed offensive star who could . . . dunk it home on sweeping, swooping drives."[2]

While he was a Sonics forward, Haywood made the All-NBA first team twice, and he made the second team twice. In 1972–73, he averaged a phenomenal 29.2 points and 12.9 rebounds per game.

Jack Sikma

In Jack Sikma's first preseason game, Houston's Moses Malone burned him for 39 points. "It was a rude awakening," Sikma said. "I realized I had a lot to learn."[3] He was a quick learner. The next week he scored 38 points of his own against Phoenix.

From 1977–78 through 1985–86, the seven-foot Sikma was Seattle's rock in the middle. "The Banger," as Sikma was known, twice led the league in defensive rebounds. He was a respected defender and noted passing whiz. In one season, he shot 92.2 percent from the free-throw line. Sikma's deadliest weapon was his unorthodox jumper. He released the shot with the ball behind his head, making it impossible to block.

Sikma finished his career in Milwaukee in the 1990–91 season. When he hung up his sneakers, he had totaled 17,287 points and 10,816 rebounds, and had played in seven All-Star Games.

Dale Ellis

"Is there a better shooter in the league?" wrote Jordan Cohn and Rick Barry.[4] Experts think long and hard before answering that question. Prior to the 1997–98 season, Dale Ellis had drained more three-pointers (1,461) than any other player in NBA history. And he canned them at a sensational 40 percent clip.

After languishing on the Dallas Mavericks bench for three years, Ellis was dealt to Seattle in 1986. Given the chance to play, he exploded for 24.9 points per game in 1986–87. In the following years he had scoring averages of 25.8, 27.5, and 23.5. He won the league's Long-Distance Shootout in 1988 and scored 27 points in the 1989 All-Star Game.

"He comes off screens, receives the ball, pfff it's on its way," wrote Cohn and Barry.[5]

The Sonics traded Ellis in 1990–91, then reacquired him in 1997. At age thirty-seven, he still had the three-point touch.

Shawn Kemp

Shawn Kemp never played college basketball. But when he unleashed one of his earth-shaking dunks as a rookie in 1989–90, fans popped out of their seats like bread out of a toaster.

"What whets everybody's appetite is his sheer physical ability," wrote Jordan Cohn and Rick Barry. "His offensive potential is, in a word, scary."[6]

Kemp simply bursts with talent. He's big (six-feet ten-inches), quick, and strong, and can jump to the

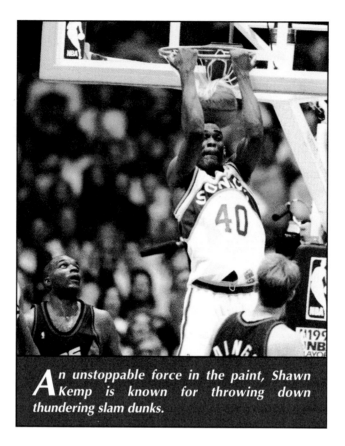

*A*n unstoppable force in the paint, Shawn Kemp is known for throwing down thundering slam dunks.

moon. When he explodes to the hoop for one of his ferocious dunks, opponents just clear out of the way.

Nicknamed Reign Man, Kemp was named to the All-NBA second-team in 1993–94, 1994–95, and 1995–96. He became Seattle's all-time shot-blocker in 1995. And in 1995–96, he averaged 19.6 points and 11.4 rebounds per game while leading the Sonics to the NBA Finals. He was traded to Cleveland in 1997.

Gary Payton

One of the best defensive guards in the NBA, Gary Payton has earned the nickname The Glove. "He

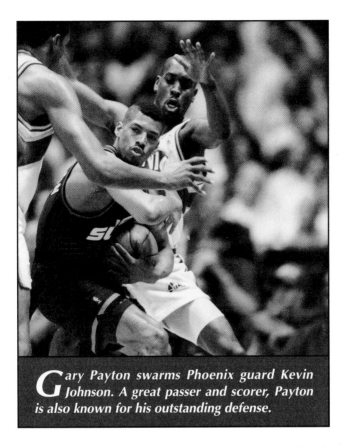

Gary Payton swarms Phoenix guard Kevin Johnson. A great passer and scorer, Payton is also known for his outstanding defense.

makes steals, forces turnovers, and generally drives opponents crazy," proclaimed *Street and Smith's Guide to Pro Basketball.*[7]

Payton began running the point for the Sonics in 1990–91 (his rookie year) and quickly led them to prominence. He's one of the NBA's top assist men, and he averaged 21.8 PPG (points per game) in 1996–97. His left-handed fallaway shot off the glass leaves defenders shaking their heads.

"I don't think any regular basketball player can stop me," Payton said.[8] And he's proved it. In NBA MVP voting, he usually finishes among the top ten.

*L*enny Wilkens has won more games than any other coach in NBA history. He is the only person to be inducted into the Basketball Hall of Fame as a pro player and pro coach.

GREAT LEADERS

O ver the years, various personalities have run the Sonics. Their most successful leaders include two former basketball legends, a pair of straight-arrow guys, and one coach who's been deemed an eccentric.

Lenny Wilkens

In 1969, Seattle general manager Dick Vertlieb approached Lenny Wilkens. He asked his point guard whether he wanted to be player/coach. Said Wilkens: "I decided, what the heck? . . . Everyone always said I was like a coach on the floor anyway."[1]

Indeed, in thirteen seasons as an NBA point guard (four with Seattle), Wilkens ran the offense like a wily quarterback. Nine times he was voted to the All-Star Game. But as a coach he reached an even higher level. Wilkens was the Sonics' player/coach from 1969–70 through 1971–72, and he was the full-time coach from

1977–78 through 1984–85. He took over a 5–17 team in 1977–78 and led it to the season's NBA Finals. He won Seattle's only world championship the next year.

Wilkens's philosophy: tough defense and a team-oriented approach. Moreover, Lenny's confidence and composure kept players relaxed and focused.

Since 1969, Wilkens has coached for Seattle, Portland, Cleveland, and Atlanta. In 1995–96, he became the first coach in NBA history to win one thousand games.

Bill Russell

On May 11, 1973, the SuperSonics announced "one of the major deals in American sports history."[2] They had hired a new coach and general manager: the legendary Bill Russell.

With extraordinary defense, rebounding, and heart, Russell had won a record 11 championships with the Boston Celtics. Two of his titles came as player/coach (1968 and 1969). In 1973, Russell joined Seattle for his first stint as a suit-and-tie head coach.

The results were mixed. In 1974–75, he led the Sonics to their first-ever playoff berth. However, like many great athletes turned coaches, Russell could not understand why players were not able to reach his standards. Players, wrote Peter Bjarkman, felt he was "distant and overbearing."[3] His record with the Sonics: a modest 162–166. Russell left Seattle in 1977.

Bernie Bickerstaff

Who would turn down an offer to play for the Harlem Globetrotters? Bernie Bickerstaff would . . . and did!

The Seattle SuperSonics Basketball Team

*F*ormer teammates Bill Russell and K. C. Jones talk prior to a game. Russell and Jones each coached the Sonics at one time.

The hard-working, no-nonsense Bickerstaff was not one for the Globetrotters' funny antics.

After graduating from San Diego University, Bickerstaff devoted his life to coaching. He coached for nearly two decades before landing the top job at Seattle in 1985–86. In 1986–87, he guided the talent-thin Sonics to the Western Conference Finals.

Bickerstaff was all business on the sidelines, demanding selfless team play. "The *I* should always be taken out of the equation," he said.[4] Nevertheless, Bickerstaff communicated well with his players—a rarity in modern pro sports.

In five years as Sonics coach, Bickerstaff went 202–208 and made the playoffs three times.

Bob Whitsitt

As general manager of the SuperSonics, Bob Whitsitt was always one step ahead of the competition. As Seattle coach George Karl put it, "He was one of the few people in this league who was thinking before other people even started to think!"[5]

A clean-cut businessman, Whitsitt became Seattle's general manager in 1986. He inherited a team that was 31–51 and gradually built it into a championship contender. Whitsitt made shrewd trades to stockpile first-round draft picks. And in 1992, he yanked Karl out of the CBA and installed him behind the Sonics' bench. Karl would become one of the premier coaches in the NBA.

In 1989, Whitsitt drafted a kid who had never played college ball. "The fans were a little upset at first, but I had a hunch about Shawn Kemp," Whitsitt said. "And it's looking like it paid off."[6]

George Karl

Was there a more innovative coach than Seattle's George Karl?

"It's Looney Tunes playing for him," said former Sonics forward Michael Cage. "He'll play any combination—four forwards and a guard, five forwards. . . . It's like he's got the other coach in a constant game of dare."[7]

Karl coached all over the map before joining Seattle in January 1992. He quickly became known as a defensive mastermind. Sonics defenders pressed, trapped, and switched all over the floor. Seattle forced

*G*eorge Karl is one of the most creative coaches in league history. He led Seattle to the Western Conference championship in 1996.

1,053 steals in 1993–94, six short of an NBA record. He is, said analyst Peter Vescey, "a technical genius."[8]

In his early days, Karl was known for his short fuse, but he tamed his temper and became one of the most respected coaches in the league. From 1992–93 through 1995–96, Seattle won more games than any other team in the NBA. He left the Sonics in 1998 with a record of 384–150 as the team's head coach.

*P*aul Silas of the Seattle SuperSonics reaches
around Indiana's Mickey Johnson to score
two points.

TERRIFIC TEAMS

Though the Sonics have won just one NBA championship, they have gone deep into the playoffs on several occasions.

1978-79

Freddie Brown could not wait for the 1979 playoffs to begin. A year earlier, Seattle had lost a seven-game marathon to Washington in the NBA Finals.

"You know it all boils down to us and Washington one more time," said Brown. "I think it will be wild and picturesque all over again."[1]

The Sonics certainly had the horses. Guards Gus Williams (19.2 PPG) and Dennis Johnson (15.9 PPG) keyed the offense and the defense. "Downtown" Brown (14.0 PPG) swished long-range bombs. Meanwhile, blond center Jack "Goldilocks" Sikma and veteran Paul "Papa Bear" Silas combined for 19 rebounds a night. Seattle won the Pacific Division (52–30) and yielded the fewest points in the league.

In the playoffs, the Sonics defeated the L.A. Lakers in five games and Phoenix in seven. They reached the Finals against—yes, indeed—Washington.

After dropping Game 1, 99–97, the Sonics won Games 2 and 3 with smothering backcourt defense. Williams and Johnson combined for 68 points in a Game 4 overtime win. The Sonics gutted out a 97–93 win in Game 5 to clinch the title. It was the first major sports championship the city of Seattle had ever won.

1986-87

In 1986–87, the Sonics limped into the playoffs with a 39–43 record. Then, to the amazement of the NBA world, they roared past Dallas and Houston to reach the Western Conference Finals.

"We went out there like warriors and surprised everybody," said forward Xavier McDaniel.[2]

The fast-breaking Sonics were the first team in history with three 23-points per game scorers: three-point bomber Dale Ellis (24.9), All-Star Game MVP Tom Chambers (23.3), and the "X-Man," McDaniel (23.0).

After getting creamed by Dallas in Game 1, 151–129, Seattle swept the series' remaining games. The Sonics then shocked the Rockets in six games. They won the opener in overtime, thanks to Chambers's nine overtime points. Seattle took Game 6 in double overtime, 128–125.

"We played clean but mean," said McDaniel. "We had something to prove and nothing to lose."[3]

Reality hit hard in the Western Conference Finals, however. Magic Johnson's Los Angeles Lakers sent the Cinderella Sonics home after four games.

1992-93

Following a 55–27 season, the SuperSonics entered the 1993 playoffs with a full arsenal. Youngsters Gary Payton and Shawn Kemp electrified the Seattle Coliseum with their dishes and dunks. Veteran gunners Ricky Pierce (18.2 PPG) and Eddie Johnson (14.4 PPG) smoked the nets. And George Karl's high-pressure defense smothered opponents into submission.

Eddie Johnson provided instant offense off the bench for the 1992–93 Sonics. Johnson won the NBA Sixth Man Award in 1989.

Nevertheless, Seattle would face three superpowers in the playoffs, and each series would go the limit.

The Sonics silenced the Utah Jazz in five games, as center Sam Perkins rained three-pointers in Game 5. Seattle faced Houston in the second round. That series went to Game 7—and then to overtime. "These two teams are so close, it's unbelievable," said Karl.[4] The Sonics prevailed when Houston's last-second shot rimmed out.

In the Western Conference Finals, Seattle won Games 2, 4, and 6 over Phoenix. Unfortunately, the Suns took all four odd-numbered games, including a 123–110 runaway in the finale. "They're the best fast-break team in the league," admitted a humble Karl. "I thought maybe we were."[5]

Though they fell one game short of the NBA Finals, it was a fulfilling season for Sonics fans. Not since 1979 had they witnessed so much playoff excitement.

1995-96

In the two previous seasons, the powerful Sonics had been eliminated from the playoffs in the first round. Critics called the team immature. The players could not argue the point.

"We were spoiled children then," Sonics forward Detlef Schrempf said in 1996. "Now we're grown-ups."[6]

In 1995–96, the determined Sonics roared to a 64–18 record. A more mature Shawn Kemp averaged 19.6 points per game and 11.4 rebounds per game. Guard Gary Payton was the NBA Defensive Player of the Year. The do-it-all Schrempf (17.1 PPG) and

*S*urrounded by three members of the New Jersey Nets, Shawn Kemp outmuscles them for the rebound.

bomber Hersey Hawkins (15.6 PPG) fueled the best offense in the Western Conference.

In the playoffs, Seattle slammed Sacramento, 3–1, swept Houston, 4–0, and gutted out a seven-game war with Utah. The Sonics dropped the first three games of the NBA Finals to the 72–10 Chicago Bulls. But after a rousing pep talk by Kemp, Seattle won Games 4 and 5. The Sonics dropped Game 6, but they won back their respect.

"The Sonics may have lost the series," wrote *Sports Illustrated*'s Phil Taylor, "but they . . . left having earned a reputation as a gallant, resilient team."[7]

*S*eattle's Vin Baker uses a wide variety of inside
scoring moves. He averaged 19.2 points per
game in 1997–98.

SONICS TODAY

The Seattle SuperSonics play in the coffee capital of the world. Throughout the 1990s, the team's play reflected that kind of high-energy kick. Players were often jumpy, on edge, and even short-tempered. The Sonics were plagued by contract squabbles and petty bickering. The team was often criticized for being upset early in the playoffs.

This team needed to chill out. It needed a leader with a soothing hand. And in 1997–98, it found him. His name: Vin Baker.

Vin Baker

On November 1, 1997, Seattle traded Shawn Kemp for Baker, a power forward with the Milwaukee Bucks. The Sonics received a three-time All-Star who is also a man of great character. The son of a minister, Baker provided leadership—and kindness. He greeted everyone with a warm smile.

"He's such a good guy, you don't want him to be disappointed in you," said Seattle guard David Wingate.[1]

With Baker as their anchor, the Sonics focused better and played inspired team basketball. Seattle cruised to 61–21 and the Pacific Division championship.

Dynamic Duo

Gary Payton, the vocal but now cheery point guard, led the way. In 1997–98, he averaged 19.2 points per contest and was in the running for the league's Defensive Player of the Year Award. Baker scored at will with dribble-drives, spin moves, reverses, and hooks. Baker also averaged 19.2 points a game while shooting 54.2 percent (fifth in the NBA).

Detlef Schrempf, the versatile small forward, poured in 15.8 points a game. Guard Hersey Hawkins added 10.5. Thirty-eight-year-old gunner Dale Ellis led the league in three-point accuracy (46.0 percent). In one stretch, he canned 24 of 29 shots from behind the arc.

Seattle opened the playoffs against the Minnesota Timberwolves. Baker, thrilled to play in his first post-season, embraced the NBA logo before Game 1. He then busted out with 14 first-quarter points, as Seattle took Game 1, 108–83. Minnesota, however, came back with two gutty victories, 98–93 and 98–90. Suddenly, the Sonics were one game away from elimination. It was a position they'd been in many times before.

"I don't think anyone deserves to live through what goes on in the next forty-eight hours," said Seattle

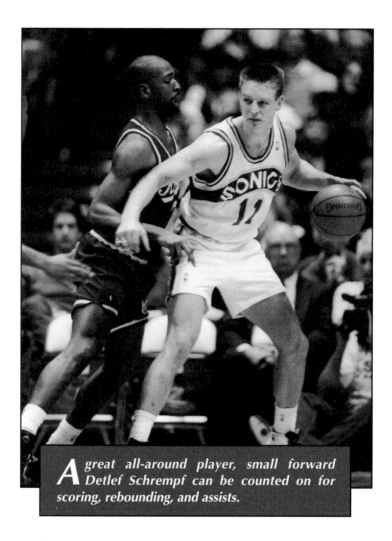

A great all-around player, small forward Detlef Schrempf can be counted on for scoring, rebounding, and assists.

coach George Karl. "Your body goes through a lot of unbelievable emotional turmoil."[2]

The Sonics, though, showed their veteran savvy. They took Game 4, 92–88, and Game 5, 97–84. In the finale, Payton rang up 29 points while never leaving the floor. "[Coach Karl] kept asking me if I could go all the way," said Payton. "I said, 'Yeah. I want to play. I want to win.'"[3]

Shackled

Next up in round two: Shaquille O'Neal and the 61–21 Los Angeles Lakers. Riding momentum, the Sonics blitzed L.A., 106–92, in Game 1. However, beginning in Game 2, dark clouds rolled into Seattle. What had been a sunny, cheery season suddenly turned black. Seattle lost Game 2, 92–68, its lowest offensive output in 193 postseason games.

In Game 3, the Sonics entered their house of doom, the Los Angeles Forum. Seattle had lost eight straight playoff games there, and this time was no different. The Lakers won, 119–103. In Game 4, the Lakers took advantage of Seattle's one weakness—lack of a physical center. O'Neal scored 39 points in a 112–100 victory. L.A. cruised in Game 5, 110–95, pulling the shade on Seattle's season.

In a sense, it was the end of an era for the Sonics. Management said good-bye to Coach Karl in May 1998. The team had six potential free agents, and Nate McMillan, a gritty role player for the Sonics for twelve years, hung up his sneakers for good. "I'm going to miss Nate," said Payton. "I hope that I can win a championship for him some day—and give him my ring."[4]

Hope For The Future

McMillan was realistic about Seattle's future. "They still have an awful lot of talent here," he said. "But they've got to find someone to match up with Shaquille because the dude is not going anywhere for several years."[5]

While management pursues its coveted big man, it takes pride in its All-Star nucleus. Through 1997–98,

The Seattle SuperSonics Basketball Team

*G*liding past fellow All-Star Mitch Richmond, Gary Payton drops in two points. Payton is the Sonics' floor leader and one of the best players in the game.

Payton, Baker, Schrempf, and Hawkins have played in a combined thirteen midseason classics. The new head coach, Paul Westphal, led Phoenix to the 1993 NBA Finals. McMillan was added to the staff as an assistant. An NBA championship—who knows? But one thing seems certain: Basketball excitement, Sonics style, will dribble on in the Great Northwest.

STATISTICS

Team Record

SEASON	SEASON RECORD	PLAYOFF RECORD	COACH	DIVISION FINISH
1967–68	23–59	—	Al Bianchi	5th
1968–69	30–52	—	Al Bianchi	6th
1969–70	36–46	—	Lenny Wilkens	5th
1970–71	38–44	—	Lenny Wilkens	4th
1971–72	47–35	—	Lenny Wilkens	3rd
1972–73	26–56	—	Tom Nissalke Bucky Buckwalter	4th
1973–74	36–46	—	Bill Russell	3rd
1974–75	43–39	4–5	Bill Russell	2nd
1975–76	43–39	2–4	Bill Russell	2nd
1976–77	40–42	—	Bill Russell	4th
1977–78	47–35	13–9	Bob Hopkins Lenny Wilkens	3rd
1978–79	52–30	12–5	Lenny Wilkens	1st
1979–80	56–26	7–8	Lenny Wilkens	2nd
1980–81	34–48	—	Lenny Wilkens	6th
1981–82	52–30	3–5	Lenny Wilkens	2nd
1982–83	48–34	0–2	Lenny Wilkens	3rd
1983–84	42–40	2–3	Lenny Wilkens	3rd
1984–85	31–51	—	Lenny Wilkens	4th (tie)
1985–86	31–51	—	Bernie Bickerstaff	5th
1986–87	39–43	7–7	Bernie Bickerstaff	4th
1987–88	44–38	2–3	Bernie Bickerstaff	3rd
1988–89	47–35	3–5	Bernie Bickerstaff	3rd
1989–90	41–41	—	Bernie Bickerstaff	4th
1990–91	41–41	2–3	K. C. Jones	5th

Team Record (con't)

SEASON	SEASON RECORD	PLAYOFF RECORD	COACH	DIVISION FINISH
1991–92	47–35	4–5	K. C. Jones Bob Kloppenburg George Karl	4th
1992–93	55–27	10–9	George Karl	2nd
1993–94	63–19	2–3	George Karl	1st
1994–95	57–25	1–3	George Karl	2nd
1995–96	64–18	13–8	George Karl	1st
1996–97	57–25	8–8	George Karl	1st
1997–98	61–21	4–6	George Karl	1st
Totals	1,371–1,171	99–101		

Coaching Records

COACH	YEARS COACHED	RECORD	CHAMPIONSHIPS
Al Bianchi	1967–69	53–111	None
Lenny Wilkens	1969–72, 1977–85	478–402	Western Conference, 1978 NBA Champions, 1979
Tom Nissalke	1972–73	13–32	None
Bucky Buckwalter	1973	13–24	None
Bill Russell	1973–77	162–166	None
Bob Hopkins	1977	5–17	None
Bernie Bickerstaff	1985–90	202–208	None
K. C. Jones	1990–91	59–59	None
Bob Kloppenburg	1991	2–2	None
George Karl	1992–98	384–150	Pacific Division, 1994, 1997, 1998 Western Conference, 1996

RECORD=Record with SuperSonics only.

Ten Great Sonics

PLAYER	SEA	YRS	G	REB	AST	BLK	STL	PTS	AVG
Fred Brown	1971–84	13	963	2,637	3,160	166*	1,149*	14,018	14.6
Tom Chambers	1983–88	16	1,107	6,703	2,283	627	885	20,049	18.1
Dale Ellis	1986–91 1997–	15	1,119	4,030	1,694	180	936	18,331	16.4
Spencer Haywood**	1970–75	12	760	7,038	1,351	629*	355*	14,592	19.2
Shawn Kemp	1989–97	9	705	6,723	1,293	1,049	883	11,590	16.4
Xavier McDaniel	1985–90	12	870	5,313	1,775	416	791	13,606	15.6
Gary Payton	1990–	8	654	2,462	4,380	139	1,494	10,419	15.9
Detlef Schrempf	1993–	13	983	6,243	3,408	266	771	14,331	14.6
Jack Sikma	1977–86	14	1,107	10,816	3,488	1,048	1,162	17,287	15.6
Lenny Wilkens	1968–72	15	1,077	5,030	7,211	26*	174*	17,772	16.5

Column group header: CAREER STATISTICS (over G, REB, AST, BLK, STL, PTS, AVG)

All stats through 1997–98 season.
*Blocks and Steals were not kept as official statistics until the 1973–74 season.
**Does not include American Basketball Association (ABA) statistics.

SEA=Seasons with SuperSonics   REB=Rebounds   STL=Steals
YRS=Years in the NBA   AST=Assists   PTS=Total points
G=Games   BLK=Blocks   AVG=Scoring average

CHAPTER NOTES

Chapter 1. The Comeback

1. Roland Lazenby, *The NBA Finals: 50th Anniversary Celebration*, 2nd ed. (Indianapolis: Masters Press, 1996), pp. 195–196.

2. Bob Logan, "'Jesse James Call' Lets Bullets Win After the Gun," *Chicago Tribune*, May 21, 1979, Sports, p. 1.

3. Ibid., p. 4.

4. Lazenby, p. 198.

5. *Complete NBA Basketball Guide* (Redmond, Wash.: Microsoft Corporation, 1996); CD-ROM: "Teams," "Seattle SuperSonics," "Team History."

6. Ted Green, "Sonics Close Out Bullets," *Los Angeles Times*, June 2, 1979, p. 6.

7. Ibid., p. 1.

Chapter 2. Colorful Characters

1. Michael E. Goodman, *Seattle SuperSonics* (Mankato, Minn.: Creative Education, Inc., 1993), n. p.

2. *Complete NBA Basketball Guide* (Redmond, Wash.: Microsoft Corporation, 1996); CD-ROM: "Teams," "Seattle SuperSonics," "Team History."

3. Peter C. Bjarkman, *The Encyclopedia of Pro Basketball Team Histories* (New York: Carroll & Graf Publishers, 1994), p. 234.

Chapter 3. Super Sonics

1. Terry Pluto, *Loose Balls* (New York: Simon & Schuster, 1990), p. 184.

2. Martin Taragano, *Basketball Biographies* (Jefferson, N.C.: McFarland & Company, Inc., 1991), p. 120.

3. *Complete NBA Basketball Guide* (Redmond, Wash.: Microsoft Corporation, 1996); CD-ROM: "Players," "Jack Sikma."

4. Rick Barry and Jordan E. Cohn, *Rick Barry's Pro Basketball Scouting Report* (Chicago: Bonus Books, Inc., 1990), p. 68.

5. Ibid., p. 69.

6. Ibid., p. 115.

7. *Street & Smith's Guide to Pro Basketball 1997–98* (New York: Ballantine Books, 1997), p. 301.

8. America Online, *The Sporting News*, "5/1: Gary Payton, Seattle SuperSonics."

Chapter 4. Great Leaders

1. *Complete NBA Basketball Guide* (Redmond, Wash.: Microsoft Corporation, 1996); CD-ROM: "Players," "Jack Sikma."

2. "Russell New Coach of Sonics," *Chicago Tribune*, May 12, 1973, Sports, p. 1.

3. Peter C. Bjarkman, *The Encyclopedia of Pro Basketball Team Histories* (New York: Carroll & Graf Publishers, 1994), p. 237.

4. *Denver Nuggets 1993–1994 Media Guide* (Denver: Denver Nuggets, 1993), p. 8.

5. Jim Moore, "Whitsitt Named Blazers GM," *Seattle Post-Intelligencer*, July 13, 1994, Sports, p. 1.

6. *Seattle SuperSonics 1992–1993 Media Guide* (Seattle: Seattle SuperSonics, 1992), p. 7.

7. Phil Taylor, "Peerless in Seattle," *Sports Illustrated*, May 2, 1994, p. 33.

8. *Seattle SuperSonics 1992–1993 Media Guide*, p. 8.

Chapter 5. Terrific Teams

1. Roland Lazenby, *The NBA Finals: 50th Anniversary Celebration*, 2nd ed. (Indianapolis: Masters Press, 1996), pp. 196–197.

2. Michael E. Goodman, *Seattle SuperSonics* (Mankato, Minn.: Creative Education, Inc., 1993), n. p.

3. Ibid.

4. Robert Falkoff, "Sonic Doom," *Houston Post*, May 23, 1993, p. B1.

5. Phil Taylor, "Flight Time," *Sports Illustrated*, June 7, 1993, p. 16.

6. Tim Crothers, "When It Counts," *Sports Illustrated*, June 3, 1996, p. 28.

7. Phil Taylor, "Vintage," *Sports Illustrated*, June 24, 1996, p. 32.

Chapter 6. Sonics Today

1. Phil Taylor, "Happy Days," *Sports Illustrated*, February 9, 1998, p. 34.

2. Scores & Stats, "Seattle SuperSonics/Minnesota Timberwolves Game Recap," April 28, 1998, <http://www.nba.com>.

3. Scores & Stats, "Seattle SuperSonics/Minnesota Timberwolves Game Recap," May 2, 1998, <http://www.nba.com>.

4. "NBA Playoffs, Western Conference," May 13, 1998, <http://cnnsi.com>.

5. Ibid.

GLOSSARY

All-Defensive first team—A team, selected by the coaches, made up of the best defensive player at each position for that season. There is also a second team.

All-NBA first team—A team, selected by basketball writers and broadcasters, made up of the best player at each position for that season.

assist—A pass to a player who soon shoots and scores.

center—This is usually the biggest player on the team, and is positioned close to the basket.

fast break—Through passing and dribbling, the offensive team races the ball downcourt toward the basket.

field goal—Any shot attempted during play (excluding free throws).

free throw—A player who is fouled is often awarded a free throw. The player shoots one or two uncontested shots from the free-throw line, which is fifteen feet from the basket.

Long-Distance Shootout—An event held the day before the NBA All-Star Game. The NBA's best three-point shooters try to score as many three-point shots as possible in a set amount of time.

point guard—The team member responsible for dribbling the ball upcourt and passing to the open teammate.

power forward—Usually a bigger player than the small forward. This position requires strong rebounding and inside scoring skills.

rebound—A grab of a missed shot that has bounced off the rim or backboard.

small forward—This player is usually counted on for both outside and inside scoring, as well as playing good perimeter defense.

SuperSonics—Nickname given to Seattle's NBA expansion team in 1967. Name relates to the city's jet aircraft industry.

three-point shot—A field goal that is worth three points. The shot is taken behind the three-point line, which ranges from 22 feet to 23 feet, 9 inches from the basket.

FURTHER READING

Bjarkman, Peter C. *The Encyclopedia of Pro Basketball Team Histories*. New York: Carroll & Graf, 1994.

Clary, Jack. *The NBA: Today's Stars, Tomorrow's Legends*. New York: Smithmark Publishing, 1997.

Goodman, Michael E. *Seattle SuperSonics*. Mankato, Minn.: Creative Education, Inc., 1993.

Italia, Bob. *The Seattle SuperSonics*. Minneapolis: Abdo & Daughters, 1997.

Knapp, Ron. *Top 10 Professional Basketball Coaches*. Springfield, N.J.: Enslow Publishers, Inc., 1998.

Lazenby, Roland. *The NBA Finals: 50th Anniversary Celebration*. Second edition. Indianapolis: Masters Press, 1996.

Rousso, Nick. *Basketball Legends*. Lincolnwood, Ill.: Publications International, Ltd., 1996.

Sachare, Alex, ed. *The Official NBA Basketball Encyclopedia*. New York: Villard Books, 1994.

Sampson, Curt. *Full Court Pressure*. New York: Doubleday & Company, 1995.

Taragano, Martin. *Basketball Biographies*. Jefferson, N.C.: McFarland & Company, Inc., 1991.

Thornley, Stew. *Shawn Kemp: Star Forward*. Springfield, N.J.: Enslow Publishers, Inc., 1998.

Torres, John Albert. *Top 10 Basketball Three-Point Shooters*. Springfield, N.J.: Enslow Publishers, Inc., 1999.

Vancil, Mark, ed. *The NBA at Fifty*. West Haven, Conn.: Park Lane, 1996.

Vancil, Mark and Don Jozwiak. *NBA Basketball: An Official Fan's Guide*. Chicago: Triumph Books, 1997.

INDEX

WHERE TO WRITE

Seattle SuperSonics
190 Queen Anne Avenue
Suite 200
Seattle, WA 98109

WEBSITE

http://www.nba.com/sonics
http://espn.go.com/nba/clubhouses/sea.html

The Seattle SuperSonics Basketball Team